ASK GOD

Becoming Comfortable Asking God Questions

ASK GOD

Becoming Comfortable Asking God Questions

SANDRA CALLOWAY FIELDS

Copyright © 2022 by Sandra Calloway Fields
Published by Glimpse of Glory Christian Book Publishing
ISBN: 978-1-7364667-42

Printed in the United States of America

All rights reserved. No part of this publication may be reproduced, stored in a retrieval system or transmitted, in any form, or by any means, electronic, mechanical, recorded, photocopied, or otherwise, without the prior permission of the copyright owner, except by a reviewer who may quote brief passages in a review.

Unless otherwise identified, scripture quotations are from King James Version, New King James Version. Scriptures marked "KJV" are taken from the King James Version (KJV): King James Version, public domain.

Scripture quotations marked (NLT) are taken from the Holy Bible, New Living Translation, copyright © 1996, 2004, 2015 by Tyndale House Foundation. Used by permission of Tyndale House Publishers. Carol Stream, Illinois 60188. All rights reserved.

Scripture quotations marked (NIV) are taken from the Holy Bible, New International Version ®, NIV®. Copyright © 1973, 1978, 1984, 2011 by Biblica, Inc. ™ used by permission of Zondervan. All rights reserved worldwide. www.zondervan.com. The "NIV" and "New International Version" are trademarks registered in the United States Patent and Trademark Office by Biblica, Inc. ™

Scripture quotations marked MSG are taken from The Message, copyright © 1993, 2002, 2018 by Eugene H. Peterson. Used by permission of NavPress. All rights reserved. Represented by Tyndale House Publishers.

Scripture quotations marked TPT are from The Passion Translation ®. Copyright © 2017, 2018, 2020 by Passion and Fire Ministries, Inc. Used by permission. All rights reserved. ThePassionTranslation.com.

Scripture quotations taken from the Amplified® Bible (AMP), Copyright ©2015 by The Lockman Foundation. Used by permission. www.lockman.org.

TABLE OF CONTENTS

Introduction 7
   Chapter 1: God, Why Am I Here? 9
   Chapter 2: God, What is Your Purpose and Plans for My Life? 15
   Chapter 3: God, How Do I Trust You in Difficult Times? 19
   Chapter 4: God, Why Should I Have a Prayer Life? 23
   Chapter 5: God, How Can I Glorify You? 25
   Chapter 6: God, Is Forgiveness for Me? 33
   Chapter 7: God, Is Heaven and Hell Real? 35
   Chapter 8: God, Will I Ever See My Loved Ones Again Who Have Transitioned? 37
   Journal 43

INTRODUCTION

There are tons of questions clashing in our brains every second of the day. Some of those questions we find ourselves asking people and some of those questions we find ourselves asking God. Interestingly, I have learned that some people are afraid to ask God questions. Are you that person? Perhaps someone told you that you should never question God, so every single time you attempt to ask Him a question you feel very uncomfortable. I really want you to understand that many of us are curious human beings, so it is clearly not wrong or uncommon for any of us to ask Him questions throughout our lives.

I have asked God many questions up to this point in my life, and He has answered every single one of them. I can assure you that He will answer the questions you ask Him, too. He can answer your questions through many forms. He can answer your questions through a vision or a dream. He can also answer your questions through a sermon that your pastor may preach at a Sunday service or at a midweek Bible Study service. He can answer your questions through His Word, the Bible. Wikipedia defines the Bible as "a collection of sacred texts or scriptures that is a product of divine inspiration and a record of the relationship between God and humans."

Over the years, I have read the Bible and, by doing so, God has given me insight, expanded my understanding and knowledge, increased my faith, and revealed so many things to me. As you read this book, you will find questions that I have asked God before, along with some questions you may have asked Him or thought about asking Him.

God did create us in his image, right? Therefore, I would like you to explore the questions of our humanity. I would like for you to search deep inside your soul and pull those questions out that you have been wanting to ask God. I want you to know that by asking questions you can discover who you are. Yes, God will reveal some things to you about yourself. It is great when God shows us things about ourselves, because it gives us an opportunity to change.

With God's grace, I will guide you in this book and provide scriptures to help answer some of the questions you have been asking Him or desiring to ask Him. It is my sincere hope and prayer that God will open your eyes and mind and give you wisdom to journey with Him as He reveals many things to you throughout this book.

CHAPTER 1

God, Why Am I Here?

Have you ever asked God why you are here? I have. I know that I am a product of my parents' love for each other, but I wanted to know why I existed as a child, especially after having a near-death experience at the age of five. I had not even been on the earth long and I faced something that I will never forget. One day, I was in my bedroom playing with my dolls when my little brother called my name, and I left my bedroom to go see what he wanted. He said that he had something he wanted to show me. It was a newspaper rolled tightly in his tiny hands. "Look what I can do," he said while smiling from ear to ear. Then he stooped down by the gas furnace and lit the newspaper on fire. I quickly ran back into my bedroom, and he chased after me. When he swung at me with the fiery newspaper, he missed me and struck the white sheets on my bed instead. Those sheets ignited quickly. I panicked and stood there for a moment trying to quickly think of what to do. The first thing that came to mind was to hide under my bed, so I did. My brother also thought it was a good idea to hide under the bed beside me.

My brother and I were both scared. I was so nervous and afraid to see the fire that filled the entire room. I remember hearing the crackling of the wood frame of the door. The grey smoke was so thick, and it was exceedingly difficult to breathe. While I was gasping for breath, it was as if everything became silent for a moment. Then, suddenly, I heard a soft voice call out my name and telling me to get up and go to the window. Although I was fearful, I recognized that was the voice of my mother, and I learned later that the voice of God was speaking to me through her, too. So, with my eyes closed, I grabbed my brother's hand and crawled out from under the bed and followed the sound of her voice as God led me. When I opened my eyes, I was in my mother's arms. My heart was racing because I was literally scared of what she would do to me. I just knew that I would get in trouble, but I didn't and neither did my brother. I did not have a scratch on me from crawling under the bed, neither did my brother. I did not get burned, neither did my brother. The whole house ended up burning, but my entire family made it out of the house safely and we were all in one piece, just as if nothing ever happened.

Now if that wasn't enough to encounter after only being in this world for five years, let me share what happened to me 33 years later. I experience something that nearly turned my world upside down. That something could have easily caused me to die during that time, but I survived what was meant to destroy me, which made me realize even more why God made me and why I am still here on the earth amongst the living.

I was 38 years old when I learned that I had ovarian cancer. I was told that I would have to have surgery to remove the cancer, and I did. While recovering from the surgery, not even a month later, I found a lump in my right breast. Sadly, the doctors informed me that I had stage four metastatic breast cancer. My ears had heard enough. This was the kind of news I wouldn't have wanted anyone else in the world to hear. I was sad, hurt, shocked, and in pain. Despite how I was feeling, I had to keep believing, keep hoping, keep praying, and keep moving forward.

My doctors informed me of a treatment plan, and I followed their plan. I had to have radiation treatment. I underwent 36 double doses of radiation on my right breast, had a lumpectomy, and reconstruction on that same breast. The radiation affected both of my hips; therefore, I had to have two surgeries to have them replaced. I had one hip replaced in 2019 and the other one in 2020.

Even though I was mentally, emotionally, and physically drained after having those surgeries, along with losing my hair three times, I had to literally muster up enough strength to stand up in the spirit and in the natural to love myself, build myself up, speak life into myself, minister to myself, and encourage myself. There were days when I would stand in the bathroom and just look at myself in the mirror. While looking in the mirror, I would see a reflection of my scars and I would say, "God, I am thankful I'm still standing." I remember those times I used to try on different wigs while looking in that same mirror, and I would say to myself, "You are so pretty." I have had to consistently remain positive and say positive things to myself ever since.

As I reflect upon what I encountered at the age of five and the age of 38, I know that God was in the burning house with me, and He was in the surgery room with me during every surgery. He was also with me in other situations that I encountered from childhood to this point in my life. He saved my life for a time such as now. And I am happy to be alive to share my story of hope, healing, restoration, and more in this season of my life. I know that I am here for a reason far greater than I could possibly comprehend. I know that I am purposed to make a difference in this world. I want you to know that you are also here for a reason, and you are purposed to make a difference, too. If you look back over your life, I am certain you have had ups and downs, "have had hills to climb," gone through trials and tribulations, and so much more. God has had His hands on your life. He kept you just like He kept me.

I would like to share some scriptures that have helped me understand why I am here. These scriptures can also help you. Allow me to insert this nugget: Every person that God used in the Bible went through something, and that something was not easy. But God got the Glory out of their story.

Daniel 3:19-29 MSG
Nebuchadnezzar, his face purple with anger, cut off Shadrach, Meshach, and Abednego. He ordered the furnace fired up seven times hotter than usual. He ordered some strong men from the army to tie them up, hands and feet, and throw them into the roaring furnace. Shadrach, Meshach, and Abednego, bound hand and foot, fully dressed from head to toe, were pitched into the roaring fire. Because the king was in such a hurry and the furnace was so hot, flames from the furnace killed the men who carried Shadrach, Meshach, and Abednego to it, while the fire raged around Shadrach, Meshach, and Abednego. Suddenly King Nebuchadnezzar jumped up in alarm and said, "Didn't we throw three men, bound hand and foot, into the fire?" "That's right, O king," they said. "But look!" he said. "I see four men, walking around freely in the fire, completely unharmed! And the fourth man looks like a son of the gods!" Nebuchadnezzar went to the door of the roaring furnace and called in, "Shadrach, Meshach, and Abednego, servants of the High God, come out here!" Shadrach, Meshach, and Abednego walked out of the fire... All the important people, the

government leaders and king's counselors, gathered around to examine them and discovered that the fire hadn't so much as touched the three men—not a hair singed, not a scorch mark on their clothes, not even the smell of fire on them! Nebuchadnezzar said, "Blessed be the God of Shadrach, Meshach, and Abednego! He sent his angel and rescued his servants who trusted in him! They ignored the king's orders and laid their bodies on the line rather than serve or worship any god but their own. "Therefore, I issue this decree: Anyone anywhere, of any race, col or, or creed, who says anything against the God of Shadrach, Meshach, and Abednego will be ripped to pieces, limb from limb, and their houses torn down. There has never been a god who can pull off a rescue like this."

Psalm 30:3 TPT
You brought me back from the brink of death, from the depths below. Now here I am, alive and well, fully restored!

Psalm 86:11-13 TPT
Teach me more about you, how you work and how you move, so that I can walk onward in your truth until everything within me brings honor to your name. With all my heart and passion, I will thank you, my God! I will give glory to your name, always and forever! You love me so much and you placed your greatness upon me. You rescued me from the deepest place of darkness, and you have delivered me from a certain death.

John 10:10 NIV
The thief comes only to steal and kill and destroy; I have come that they may have life and have it to the full.

Psalm 5:7-8 MSG
And here I am, your invited guest— it is incredible! I enter your house; here I am, prostrate in your inner sanctum, waiting for directions to get me safely through enemy lines.

CHAPTER 2

God, What Is Your Purpose and Plans for My Life?

Some people do not feel like they have a purpose in life. They don't feel like God can use them. They feel unworthy. They feel rejected. They feel hopeless. They feel unimportant. They feel like an outcast. They feel underserving. They feel unqualified. They feel like others are superior to them. They even feel like they need the approval of others to do something that God has placed upon their hearts. If you are one of those people, I want you to know that God has anointed and appointed each of us with and for purpose while we are here on the earth. And that settles it. "You are enough" for God to use for His Glory.

God has found you worthy to carry out your purpose. Only you can carry out what He has purposed you to do on this earth. Only you can touch and make a difference in the lives of the people He intends for you to reach. Only you can go into certain territories to complete certain assignments that will bring Him glory. Only you and no one else. Your life is "purpose-driven," so therefore God is going to use you to make a major difference in this world. You were already chosen to do that something before you were even thought about being conceived in your mother's womb. Your purpose might seem small in the eyes of others, and you might even think it is small, but you must understand that your purpose is major in the eyes of God.

I often wondered what God wanted me to do in this gigantic world. I knew that there had to be something He wanted me to do, especially with all that I have gone through in my life. I remember praying day in and day out and seeking God's answers about my purpose, and He eventually revealed it to me. I did not know that by the time I turned 48 I would be an advocate for cancer patients, speaking life into those who God allows to cross my path. What an amazing purpose to have! God literally used my cancer diagnosis and the pain I endured with it to reveal what He has anointed, appointed, validated, and gifted me to do on the earth. He used the pain that I endured to catapult me. He used the pain that I endured to help others navigate through the pain they may experience on their journey.

God's purpose for our lives is so much more than anything we will ever encounter on our journey. I have learned that some of us must go through painful things, which in turn helps us give birth to our purpose. Think about the life of Jesus and all the pain He had to endure. His purpose was far greater than the pain He had to bear—the pain for all of us. He went to the cross and it was finished. Now we are all here to carry out our purpose and finish our work.

God's Plans

God's plans for your life will often unfold as you carry out your purpose. God's plans for your life are major. His plans for your life are real. His plans for your life are sure and set in stone. His plans for your life cannot be altered. His plans for your life will produce greatness. His plans for your life do not need anyone's validation. His plans will always transcend your own plans. So, don't get so comfortable with only doing what you want to do.

Some of us have our own personal agenda. We already have things mapped out on paper and even in our minds, without asking God what His will is for our lives. Sometimes when things don't happen the way we feel they should, at the time we feel that it should, we nag and complain, we get frustrated, we lose hope, and we are quick to give up. If you are that person who has been trying to follow your own plans for the longest, and you have experienced things not working out for you, I would like to encourage you to have confidence in knowing that God has your life mapped out and He wants you to follow His plan for your life, not your own. He wants you to fully trust Him and His process. The Bible clearly tells us to "Trust in the Lord with all thine heart and lean not unto thine own understanding. In all thy ways acknowledge him, and he shall direct thy paths" (Proverbs 3:5-6 KJV).

God will teach you, instruct you, and make sure that His plans for your life are carried out. You will not only need to trust Him, but you will also need to listen to Him and obey Him, because He is the best teacher and leader that any of us could ever have. His Word declares, "If ye be willing and obedient, ye shall eat the good of the land" (Isaiah 1:19 KJV). When you obey God, you will not have to worry about things not working out for you. You will see with your own eyes how things "will work together for your good," just how God intends for it to happen.

I would like to share some scriptures that have helped me understand my purpose as well as some of God's plans for my life. These scriptures can also help you.

Proverbs 19:21 NIV
Many are the plans in a person's heart, but it is the Lord's purpose that prevails.

Jeremiah 1:5 NIV
Before I formed you in the womb I knew you, before you were born, I set you apart; I appointed you as a prophet to the nations.

Jeremiah 29: 11 KJV
For I know the thoughts that I think toward you, saith the Lord, thoughts of peace, and not of evil, to give you an expected end.

Isaiah 43:7 AMP
Everyone who is called by My Name, Whom I have created for My glory, Whom I have formed, even whom I have made.

Isaiah 14:24 NIV
The Lord Almighty has sworn, "Surely, as I have planned, so it will be, and as I have purposed, so it will happen."

Psalm 138:8 AMP
The Lord will accomplish that which concerns me; Your unwavering lovingkindness, O Lord, endures forever—Do not abandon the works of Your own hands.

CHAPTER 3

God, How Do I Trust You in Difficult Times?

It is certainly not uncommon to trust God when everything in your life is good. When you have money in your pocket. When you have a job with a great salary that allows you to pay your bills and frequently do something nice for yourself. When your health is great. When you have an apartment or a home to live in. When you have a dependable vehicle to drive to various places you need to go daily. When you have clothes to wear. When your relationships and friendships are good. When there are no signs of any kind of storm coming your way. Yes, each of us can easily trust Him in the good times.

But, what about when something bad happens and you experience difficult times? You see, each of us has encountered or will encounter a difficult situation on our journey in life. Have you ever felt like you were in a pit and had no one to pull you out of it? Have you ever been so sick to the point you could barely do anything for yourself? Have you ever experienced financial lack as a result of losing a job or something else? Have you ever been homeless? Have you ever been betrayed by a friend or a family member that you thought loved you and had your back? If you answered yes to any of these questions, do you feel like you were still able to trust God to bring you through those difficult situations?

You may have heard someone say and respond to difficult situations as "life happens." Whether it is you or them going through a difficult time or season in their life, some things just happen and in such a way that can have you wondering if God really cares about what you are dealing with. Allow me to share this: God does care about everything that concerns you.

I want you to know that God has a way of testing our faith and our ability to trust Him to do for us what we need Him to do at any given time throughout our life. It is not uncommon for Him to test us when we encounter some difficult situations. As a matter of fact, He will allow things to happen just to see if we are going to seek Him and trust only Him.

You or someone you know might be facing a difficult situation right now and that situation seems to be getting the best of you, seemingly making it hard to even trust Him enough to bring you out of it. You are not alone. I have been there before. It was a very difficult time when I was diagnosed with cancer. My emotions were all over the place. When cancer tried to get the best of me, I had no choice but to lean and depend on God at that time. Honestly, I could not rely on anyone else (the doctors, family members, friends, etc.) to heal me and save my life but the One who gave me life in the first place. I had no choice but to trust God with every fiber of my being. I had to hold on to the little faith that I had at that time.

I am not going to say that it was easy to trust Him immediately after hearing such bad news about having cancer, followed by having to have several surgeries. I had to grow into building my faith to where it is now and trusting Him. Over the years, I have learned to trust God when I cannot trace Him, when I don't feel His presence, and when I don't even know what the outcome of a situation will be. I encourage you to do this very same thing. You need to work on trusting God the best you can.

One thing that is for certain is that God is still the same One who will be there for you and me during the good times and the difficult times. He will never fail any of His children. He will never forsake any of His children. He will never put more on any of us than we can truly handle. He will never expect anyone else to do what only He can do. He is fully capable of doing whatever each of us needs Him to do. Ephesians 3:20 NLT says, "Now all glory to God, who is able, through his mighty power at work within us, to accomplish infinitely more than we might ask or think."

I would like to share some scriptures that have helped me learn how to trust God and activate my faith. These scriptures can also help you.

Mark 9:23 NIV
"If you can?" said Jesus. "Everything is possible for one who believes."

Psalm 9:10 NIV
Those who know your name trust in you, for you, Lord, have never forsaken those who seek you.

Psalm 46:10 NLT
Be still and know that I am God.

Psalm 118:8 NIV
It is better to take refuge in the Lord than to trust in humans.

Psalm 20:7 NIV
Some trust in chariots and some in horses, but we trust in the name of the Lord our God.

Jeremiah 17:7 NIV
Blessed is the one who trusts in the Lord, whose confidence is in Him. They will be like a tree planted by the water that sends out its roots by the stream. It does not fear when heat comes; its leaves are always green. It has no worries in a year of drought and never fails to bear fruit.

CHAPTER 4

God, Why Should I Have a Prayer Life?

Prayer is when you communicate and have a conversation directly with God at any given time; it is to "make your request known unto Him and give thanks to Him while doing so." I want you to know that when you commit to having a relationship with God and your relationship with Him grows, you will develop a prayer life.

It is very important and necessary for every Christian to have a prayer life, and a consistent one where you commit to praying daily for yourself, your loved ones, your friends, and others. None of us can afford not to have a prayer life, especially with us being surrounded by so much evil, hatred, anger, darkness, death, and more in today's world. One thing I want you to understand is that it is not very easy to navigate through spiritual warfare, trials and tribulations, obstacles, setbacks, sickness and disease, depression, oppression, the ups and downs and pitfalls of life, without having a prayer life. You need it.

You can use prayer as a spiritual weapon. You need this spiritual weapon daily to fight that enemy called the devil. The Bible tells us that the devil walks the earth like a roaring lion, seeking whom he may devour (Read 1 Peter 5:8). The devil is very crafty and sneaky, and he will attempt to catch you off-guard and launch his attacks on you, and your family, too. He will attack every part of your life with a goal to destroy you. The devil first tried to destroy me in a house fire when I was five years old. I knew very little about praying then, but my mother certainly knew how to pray; therefore, her prayer life was a "lifeline" for me and my family when death was staring us in the face. Oh, how powerful prayer is!

I once heard someone say that "prayer also changes things," and I now know that to be true because prayer changed my life. Prayer can change your life. When you are in some of the worst seasons of your life, no matter what that season may look or feel like, you can pray your way through it. I can assure you that God will not only hear your prayers, but He will also answer every one of them.

I would like to share some scriptures that have helped me understand why having a prayer life is so important and necessary. These scriptures can also help you.

Luke 11:2-4 NIV
He said to them, "When you pray, say: "Father, hallowed be your name, your kingdom come. Give us each day our daily bread. Forgive us our sins, for we also forgive everyone who sins against us. And lead us not into temptation.

Jeremiah 29:12 NIV
Then you will call on me and come and pray to me, and I will listen to you.

Luke 6:12 NIV
One of those days, Jesus went out to a mountainside to pray, and spent the night praying to God.

James 5:13 NIV
Is anyone among you in trouble? Let them pray.

CHAPTER 5

God, How Can I Glorify You?

God's desire is for us Christians to walk upright and glorify Him in all that we do on the earth. It pleases Him when we make up in our minds to put Him first. I believe it makes Him smile anytime any of us declare with our mouth, "Glory be to God," "I give God the Glory," "All the Glory belongs to Him," "He gets the Glory, and "I will Glorify Him in all that I do." When you say one of these or even put into words another way to simply say that you glorify God, you are showing Him that you are taking absolutely no credit for what He alone has done in your life and will do in your life. When you Glorify Him, you are willing to yield every part of yourself to Him for His use. You are willing to do whatever it takes to honor and please Him first.

I remember asking God how we as Christians can glorify Him, and He revealed to me some important things that you and I need to do. Those things include being a servant of God, walking by faith and not by sight, praising and worshipping Him, obeying Him, praying to Him about everything, loving others, submitting to His will, and more.

Being a Servant of God

It is an honor and a privilege to be a servant of God; this is marvelous in His sight. When you commit to having a relationship with God, and as your relationship with Him grows, you will learn how to not only serve Him wholeheartedly, but you will also learn how to serve others well. You will selfishly serve others without expecting absolutely anything in return. Some people have the gift to serve. If you are one of those people, make sure you consistently serve with all your heart.

When you serve others, you are showing a piece of God's heart. When people see you, they should clearly see God in you; they should feel His love "flowing from your heart." And one of the ways others can see Him in you is through your service. If you have found yourself struggling with serving others, I am fully persuaded that God will help you. Really get to know Him and learn of His wonderful attributes.

Walking by Faith and Not by Sight

Merriam-Webster dictionary defines faith as a) belief or trust in and loyalty to God, and b) firm belief in something for which there is no proof. Now according to the Bible, "Faith is the substance of things hoped for, the evidence of things not seen" (Hebrews 11:1 KJV). Having faith may not always be an easy thing to do, especially when you are facing a crisis in your life, but having faith is one of the things that make our Heavenly Father move for us, in any given situation. There will be times that God will move quickly for you when He sees that you are full of faith.

And as I shared before, I want you to understand that your faith will be tested from time to time. Sometimes you will go through things in life that God will use to grow your faith. You may very well only start off with a small level of faith (the Bible mentions having faith the size of a mustard seed) until it grows exceedingly, and the growing part is sure to happen when you start studying, reading, and hearing His Word more. Try doing these things daily.

It is not the will of God for any of us to lead a faithless life. He wants us to always have "faith over fear." As I think back to when my brother and I were trapped in our burning bedroom seemingly without a way to escape, scared and fearful of what would happen next, the calmness of the voice of my mother; and the voice of God gave us strength to climb out the window. It was that experience that taught me how to activate my faith. I had faith in God without really knowing much about Him at the age of five. I was just a child yielding to His will.

Praising and Worshipping God

As a Christian, you should make it a priority to praise and worship God, and not just on the day you attend church. This is something you should gladly do every day. You should carve time out of your schedule every day of the week to get into the presence of God. Regardless of the highs and lows, the ups and downs, the good and the bad, and the trials and the tribulations that you may face on your journey, you still must push through and praise and worship God. Use those trying times in your life to praise Him more and more, and worship Him more and more. His Word tells us that we must worship Him in spirit and in truth" (John 4:24 KJV).

I believe when any of us praise and worship God, it causes the doors and windows of Heaven to be opened. I believe we will get God's attention when we praise and worship Him, because it honors Him and brings Him glory when we consistently do these things.

Obeying God

God wants each of us to lead a life of obedience. Why? Because it brings Him honor and it can bring us unlimited blessings. Again, His Word tells us that if we are willing and obedient, we will eat the good of the land. When we obey Him, His Word, His instructions, He will allow us to experience His goodness and He will reward us with nearly anything our heart desires.

I must admit that I haven't always been obedient. There were times that I disobeyed God and I had to face negative consequences. Perhaps you or someone you know may have had a moment in your life where you did not obey God either. I am certain that you, too, had to face some hard trials because of your disobedience. As Christians, we need to strive daily to live out a life of obedience. When we do, we will see just how rewarding it is.

Pray to Him About Everything

The Bible encourages each of us to "pray without ceasing" (1 Thessalonians 5:17 KJV). I know at times having to deal with the cares of the world will make you feel like you don't even need to pray, or your prayer will not help the situation at hand. But you must still pray. One psalmist sang, "Take it to God in prayer." Do not take only one thing to God in prayer, take everything to Him in prayer. Yes, every problem, every situation, every circumstance, and everything in between. I want you to know that your prayers matter, God hears them, and He will respond and answer them. And let me assure you that prayer works, so never cease to pray.

Loving Others

Many people in the world have declared how much they love the

Lord, but some of those same people have bitterness, strife, envy, jealousy, unforgiveness, and hatred in their hearts toward others. The Bible clearly tells us "If anyone boasts, "I love God," and goes right on hating his brother or sister, thinking nothing of it, he is a liar. If he won't love the person he can see, how can he love the God he can't see? The command we have from Christ is blunt: Loving God includes loving people. You've got to love both" (1 John 4:20 NLT).

None of us need anything within our hearts that will hinder us from loving others; that is why it is necessary to pray and ask God to search within our hearts and remove anything that is not like Him, anything that would hinder us from loving others the way He has commanded us to do. When we love each other unconditionally, we are exemplifying the second greatest commandment, which is "Thou shalt love thy neighbor as thyself" (Read Matthew 22:39 KJV).

Submitting to His Will

For some of us it is simply easy to submit to the will of God, but for some it is difficult. I have come to conclude that some people just want to do things their way. If you are one of those people, it is time to stop doing any and everything your way and do things God's way. You must learn to surrender your will to His because His will is right and perfect. It is time to allow Him to order your steps so you will end up "in the right place at the right time."

When you come to that place in your life where you can surrender your all to Him and tell Him "Not my will but your will be done," you have now set yourself up for greatness in every area of your life.

You might ask, How is that so? It is so because now you are in His will.

I would like to share some scriptures that have helped me learn what it means to glorify God. These scriptures can also help you.

Matthew 23:11 NIV
The greatest among you will be your servant.

2 Corinthians 6:8 NLT
We serve God whether people honor us or despise us, whether they slander us or praise us. We are honest, but they call us impostors.

Romans 12:11 NLT
Never be lazy but work hard and serve the Lord enthusiastically.

Romans 12:7 NLT
If your gift is serving others, serve them well. If you are a teacher, teach well.

Psalm 66:4 KJV
All the earth shall worship thee and shall sing unto thee; they shall sing to thy name, Selah.

Romans 10:17 KJV
So, then faith cometh by hearing, and hearing by the Word of God.

Hebrews 11:6 KJV
But without faith it is impossible to please him: for he that cometh to God must believe that he is, and that he is a rewarder of them that diligently seek him.

Romans 6:13 NLT
Do not let any part of your body become an instrument of evil to serve sin. Instead, give yourselves completely to God, for you were dead, but now you have new life. So, use your whole body as an instrument to do what is right.

Hebrews 11:8 TPT
Faith motivated Abraham to obey God's call and leave the familiar to discover the territory he was destined to inherit from God. So, he left with only a promise and without even knowing ahead of time where he was going, Abraham stepped out in faith.

Micah 6:8 MSG
But he has already made it plain how to live, what to do, what God is looking for in men and women. It is quite simple: Do what is fair and just to your neighbor, be compassionate and loyal in your love, and do not take yourself too seriously—take God seriously.

1 John 1:6-7 MSG
If we claim that we experience a shared life with him and continue to stumble around in the dark, we are obviously lying through our teeth—we are not living what we claim. But if we walk in the light, God himself being the light, we also experience a shared life with one another, as the sacrificed blood of Jesus, God's Son, purges all our sin.

Romans 14:11 KJV
For it is written, As I live, saith the Lord, every knee shall bow to me, and every tongue shall confess to God.

Isaiah 1:19 NIV
If you are willing and obedient, you will eat the good things of the land.

John 6:38 NIV
For I have come down from heaven not to do my will but to do the will of him who sent me.

Mark 3:31-35 NIV
Then Jesus' mother and brothers arrived. Standing outside, they sent someone in to call him. A crowd was sitting around him, and

they told him, "Your mother and brothers are outside looking for you." "Who are my mother and my brothers?" Then he looked at those sitting in a circle around him and said, "Here are my mother and my brothers! Whoever does God's will is my bother…and my mother."

CHAPTER 6

God, Is Forgiveness for Me?

How many times have you sinned? How many times have you hurt someone's feelings? How many times have you betrayed someone? How many times have you told yourself that you were not going to do this or that again, but you did it anyway? How many times have you fallen short of the glory of God? Have you ever felt like you would not be forgiven for something that you did wrong?

Well, if you have ever done something wrong and wondered if you would be forgiven, the answer is yes. Forgiveness is for all of God's children, not just some of His children. Now, God does not reward any of us for our wrongdoings and sins, but He loves us so much to forgive us. When God forgives you, He will not remind you of what you have done wrong like some people might do, and He does not want you to condemn yourself, beat yourself up spiritually, or dwell on whatever that something is that He forgave you for. Don't allow it to take up space in your mind and rob you of your peace any longer. He knows that all of us have faults and we will fall short sometimes. That is why He said that "His grace is sufficient."

Speaking of grace, God showed grace towards you when He forgave you, and He wants you to extend grace to others and forgive them when they have transgressed against you. It is a huge deal when you can forgive someone who has offended you or hurt you.

There is power, love, joy, and peace in forgiveness. So, forgive quickly so you will be forgiven quickly.

I would like to share some scriptures that have helped me understand the importance of forgiveness. These scriptures can also help you.

Isaiah 43:25 NIV
I, even I, am he who blots out your transgressions, for my own sake, and remembers your sins no more.

1 John 1:19 NIV
If we confess our sins, he is faithful and just and will forgive us our sins and purify us from all unrighteouness.

Acts 3:19 NIV
Repent, then, and turn to God, so that your sins may be wiped out, that times of refreshing may come from the Lord.

Ephesians 4:32 NIV
Be kind and compassionate to one another, forgiving each other, just as Christ God forgave you.

Matthew 6:14-15 NIV
For if you forgive other people when they sin against you, your heavenly Father will also forgive you. But if you do not forgive others their sins, your Father will not forgive your sins.

CHAPTER 7

God, Is Heaven or Hell Real?

Many people across the globe have wondered about "Heaven and Hell." Some believe neither exist while others believe both exist. I am one of those who believe both exist. Jesus told us that He was going to prepare a place for us, His children, and that place is called Heaven, our eternal home. It is a real place where His children can rest after departing this earth. That is amazing, isn't it?

I believe that both my mother and father who have passed away are resting in Heaven, the same place that I am looking forward to spending eternity after my time on earth expires. It is a place where any child of God should desire to go. None of us should allow anything or anyone to stand in the way of us getting there and hearing God say, "Well done good and faithful servant" (Matthew 25:23 KJV).

Each of us should live our life in such a way, steering away from sin, repenting daily, walking in love and forgiveness, and doing the other things that please God, so when we depart this earth; we will open our eyes in Heaven. "While we live in this earthly tent, we groan with a feeling of oppression, it is not that we want to get rid of our earthly body, but that we want to have the heavenly one put on over us, so that what is mortal will be transformed by life."

(Read 2 Corinthians, Chapter 5).

Hell

Hell is a place of torment where there is a never-ending fire. Hell is where the devil lives. "And the devil, who deceived them, was thrown into the lake of burning sulfur, where the beast and false prophet had been thrown. They will be tormented day and night for ever and ever" (Revelation 20:10 NIV). Each of us Christians should do all that is required of us so that hell will not end up being our destination after we depart this earth.

I would like to share some scriptures that have helped me understand that heaven and hell are both real. These scriptures can also help you.

Mark 16:19 NIV
After the Lord Jesus had spoken to them, he was taken up into heaven and he sat at the right hand of God.

Isaiah 66:1 NLT
This is what the Lord says: "Heaven is my throne, and the earth is my footstool."

2 Peter 2:4 NLT
For God did not spare even the angels who sinned. He threw them into hell, in gloomy pits of darkness, where they are being held until the day of judgment.

Mark 9:47-48 NLT
And if your eye causes you to sin, gouge it out. It's better to enter the Kingdom of God with only one eye than to have two eyes and be thrown into hell, where the maggots never die, and the fire never goes out.

CHAPTER 8

God, Will I Ever See My Loved Ones Again Who Have Transitioned?

Many people have lost loved ones and have wondered if they would ever see them again. I lost both of my parents. My father first, and then my mother. My dad, John Calloway, was a very quiet person with a warm, inviting smile. Most people called him Honest John because he was. The day that I was diagnosed with cancer, I drove to my parents' house and sat in the car and began to cry. My dad was working on the neighbor's vehicle, and he saw me weeping. He opened the passenger door of my car and began to sing "Love Lifted Me" by songwriters Howard E. Smith, James Rowe, and Michael T. Smith.

The moment he sang that song to me will always remain in my heart. It gave me hope and the will to fight. A few years later, I noticed a change in my dad's work habits. He was a very hard worker, but he began to be more attentive to his family. One day I stopped by my parents' house, and I asked my dad if everything was okay with his health, and he smiled. "I am good," he replied. He went on to say, "If your mom calls you and says that I am acting strange, just know that I am alright." The next night I received a phone call from my mom asking me to come to their house. She told me that my dad had taken her to get dinner and they sat in his old pickup truck and watched the train cars. She said that he kissed her and told her that he loved her very much, and then turned his head. And when she looked over at him again, he was smiling and in that same moment she had lost the love of her life. He had transitioned right before her eyes.

Years later, my mom passed away. My mom, Martha Calloway, was my best friend. We had a great relationship with a little spice. She was smart, demanding, and very kind. My dad told her if anything happened to him, she would stay with me. So, when he passed away, she immediately moved in with me. She had known him ever since she was nine years old, so naturally she mourned his death daily. I would hear her laughing and crying at night. I felt powerless to help ease her pain.

But I eventually did something that I thought would help her as she continued to live day by day without her soul mate. I started having girls' days out with her. We would go thrifting, to the nail shop, and different restaurants after church services. I would take her by her house, the "Pink House" as we would call it, and we would laugh and reminisce about all the fond memories we had there as a family. We started seeing the wear and tear of the house and I told her that it was time to remove it. To my surprise, she agreed. A few months later, we had a conversation and I told her that I was going to get some items out of the house before it was demolished, and seemingly out of nowhere she said, "I love you." When I returned home, I came to the door of her room and asked, "What would you like for lunch, Mom?" She did not reply. I got closer thinking she did not hear me, yet she had gotten herself dressed and had a smile on her face. The tears streamed down my face as I embraced her. I wanted her to wake up. I cried aloud and asked, "Why now, God?" Then, the thought of selfishness and anger engulfed me. I was facing the reality of losing my other parent.

Having both of my parents so many years on earth with me was a blessing from God. I know that they are in a better place—that place called Heaven. After they both transitioned, I thought, "Would I ever see them again?" If you have lost loved ones too, I am certain it has not been easy for you. I know you have had some lonely, sad, weary, and hard days. You may have also wondered if you would see your loved ones again, too.

I would like to share some scriptures that have helped me have more peace about death. These scriptures can also help you.

John 11:25-26 NIV
Jesus said to her, "I am the resurrection and the life. The one who believes in me will live, even though they die; and whoever lives by believing in me will never die. Do you believe this?

2 Corinthians 5:8 KJV
We are confident, I say, and willing rather to be absent from the body, and to be present with the Lord.

Philippians 3:20 NLT
But we are citizens of heaven, where the Lord Jesus Christ lives. And we are eagerly waiting for him to return as our Savior.

Romans 14:8 NIV
If we live, we live for the Lord; and if we die, we die for the Lord. So, whether we live or die, we belong to the Lord.

Ecclesiastes 12:7 NIV
And the dust returns to the ground it came from, and the spirit returns to God who gave it.

Dear God,

You are the only One who sees me, hears me, and knows everything about me. Thank You for seeing me right where I am, amid my pain and struggle, in the middle of my desert land. Thank You for not forgetting about me. I pray that You forgive me for not trusting You like I should have, for doubting Your goodness, and for not believing You are there. I choose to set my eyes on You today. I choose to have joy and peace. Thank You for caring for me and for loving me. I confess my need for You. Fill me fresh with Your Holy Spirit, renew my heart and my mind in Your truth. I ask for Your hope and comfort to continue to heal my heart where it has been broken. Give me the courage to face another day, knowing that with You before me and behind me, I have nothing to fear. In the Name of Jesus, Amen.

ASK GOD
JOURNAL

When God starts revealing even more things to you, write it down. If some questions you have been wanting to ask Him are not shared in this book, write them down in this journal. God wants you to become more comfortable asking Him questions and having conversations with Him.

God, Why Am I Here?

God, What is Your Purpose and Plans for My Life?

God, How Do I Trust You in Difficult Times?

God, Why Should I Have a Prayer Life?

God, How Can I Glorify You?

God, Is Forgiveness for Me?

God, Is Heaven and Hell Real?

God, Will I Ever See My Loved Ones Again Who Have Transitioned?

www.ingramcontent.com/pod-product-compliance
Lightning Source LLC
Chambersburg PA
CBHW060419050426
42449CB00009B/2029